Th

Line

(Edited selections from
Mountain, Moor and Loch
first published in 1894.)

Northern Books
from Famedram

Printed and published in Scotland by
Famedram Publishers Ltd, PO Box 3, AB41 9EA

Mountain, Moor and Loch, the source of text and drawings for this publication was published by Sir Joseph Causton & Sons in 1894, shortly after the opening of the West Highland Railway. The photographs in the text show the line as it is today .

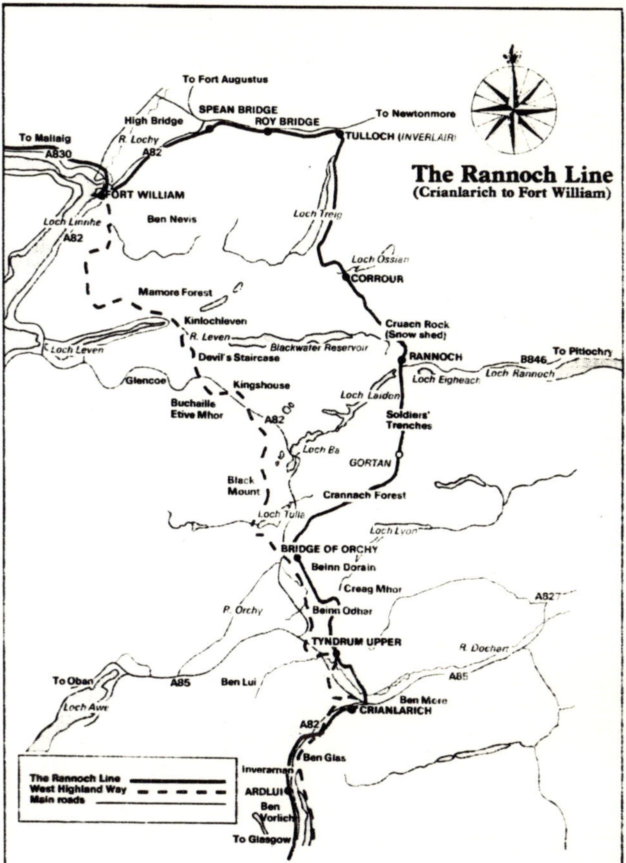

The Rannoch Line
(Crianlarich to Fort William)
To Fort Augustus
SPEAN BRIDGE
ROY BRIDGE
To Newtonmore
High Bridge
TULLOCH (INVERLAIR)
To Mallaig
R. Lochy
A830
A82
FORT WILLIAM
Ben Nevis
Loch Treig
Loch Linnhe
A82
Loch Ossian
CORROUR
Mamore Forest
Kinlochleven
Cruach Rock
(Snow shed)
R. Leven
Blackwater Reservoir
Loch Leven
Devil's Staircase
RANNOCH
B846
To Pitlochry
Loch Eigheach
Loch Rannoch
Glencoe
Kingshouse
Loch Laidon
Buchaille
Etive Mhor
A82
Soldiers'
Trenches
Loch Ba
GORTAN
Black
Mount
Crannach Forest
Loch Tulla
Loch Lyon
BRIDGE OF ORCHY
Beinn Dorain
Creag Mhor
A827
R. Orchy
Beinn Odhar
TYNDRUM UPPER
R. Dochart
To Oban
A85
Ben Lui
A85
Ben More
Loch Awe
CRIANLARICH
A82
Ben Glas
Inverarnan
The Rannoch Line
West Highland Way
Main roads
ARDLUI
Ben
Vorlich
To Glasgow

Mileages

(Crianlarich to Fort William)

Crianlarich	–
Tyndrum Upper	4¾
Bridge of Orchy	12¼
Rannoch	28
Corrour	35¼
Tulloch	45¼
Roy Bridge	51
Spean Bridge	54¼
Fort William	63½

THE RANNOCH LINE

CRIANLARICH — where the traveller who wishes to break his journey will find not only unrivalled mountain scenery, but also, what is even more essential in these wilds, a very comfortable hostelry — is the point at which the West Highland Railway, running from south to north, intersects the Callander and Oban Railway, running from east to west, the former line crossing the latter on a high viaduct. It is a little village, lying on the ridge that closes Glen Falloch, and it used to be regarded as the limit of civilisation in these parts, the Callander and Oban metals being looked on as the boundary.

All around tower grand eminences, the most notable being Ben More (3,843 feet) and Stobinian (3,827) to the east; both pyramidal mountains with flattened summits, the most lofty by 500 feet that we have yet seen. To the west lie Ben Dhu-Craig (3,204 feet) and Ben Oss (3,374), while in every quarter of the compass rise heights ranging from 2,000 to 3,000 feet. Wherever the eye wanders it is confronted by majestic hills, which seem to crowd and hustle each other into the narrow valleys, and one is reminded of Rudyard Kipling's little kingdom on the road to Thibet, which was 11,000 feet above the level of the sea and exactly four miles square, "but most of the miles stood on end owing to the nature of the country."

If a distribution of three acres and a cow were made, the cottars of such districts as that around Crianlarich would have the best of the bargain, for each man would have to be allotted a mountain with his acres, or a substantial section of one, and would be laird of half a mile of country "stood on end".

The principal "lion" of Crianlarich is, of course, Ben More; and the second is Donald Malloch, an ancient and typical Highlander, who seems to be factor, forester, gamekeeper and various other functionaries on that part of the Breadalbane property, rolled into one. The most interesting feature about this venerable and convivial Gael, is the fact that he can trace his ancestry back three thousand years, to the Prophet Malachi — a matter of distinct historical interest.

At Crianlarich the tourist is presented with as bewildering a series of alternative routes as at Arrochar and Tarbet. He can proceed northwards by the West Highland Railway, which is the course we recommend; or he can break off here and leave the remainder of the line for the return journey, going west to Oban by the Callander and Oban, thence north-east by Loch Linnhe to Fort William, and back to Crianlarich by the West Highland. If the time at his disposal does not permit of either of these attractive journeys he can strike west to Oban, passing Dalmally and the Falls of Connel, and there take the steamer back to Glasgow by way of Crinan Canal and the Kyles of Bute. If his inclination, on

Summer scenes at a busy Crianlarich in loco -hauled days

Mists roll in on Ben More as it looms over Crianlarich

Dalmally

the other hand, be eastward, he can take the Callander and Oban Railway to Killin, sail along Loch Tay to Kenmore, thence coach to Aberfeldy and take the train, via Perth, to Edinburgh or Glasgow; or from Killin he may go by rail to Lochearnhead, coach alongside Loch Earn to St Fillans and Comrie, and thence make his way by rail whither he pleases. Finally, he can go round by Callander, come through the Trossachs, thence coach to Aberfoyle and rail to Edinburgh or Glasgow, or sail along Loch Katrine, coach to Stronachlacher, sail to Tarbet and pick up the West Highland Railway at the station there — or sail to Balloch at the southern end of Loch Lomond and thence by rail to Glasgow. Each of these alternatives is tempting to the lover of the beautiful and the sublime in nature; but none of them will afford him such diversity of striking landscape than the route we have now to follow — north and west to Fort William. Wonderful as the scenery has been through which we have already passed, it is only from Crianlarich onwards that the country assumes its finest fascination: the charm of a land hitherto unexplored, a wild and lovely desert in which every frowning peak, every gleaming tarn, every stretch of brilliant moorland is a fresh surprise; a glorious waste where man is a stranger, and where there is nothing to clash with the poetry of the Creator's handiwork.

From Crianlarich, Strathfillan strikes off to the north-west, and Glen Dochart to the north-east, but the two valleys are really one, which makes a bend at Crianlarich. It is threaded all the way by a single stream, which is called the Fillan at first, and afterwards the Dochart, as it approaches the Loch of that name.

The course of the West Highland Railway is up Strathfillan, running almost parallel with the Callander and Oban for about five miles. The two diverge at Tyndrum, the former going north, and the latter west. After crossing the Fillan, but before Tyndrum Station is reached, two very interesting points are passed, first, the ancient church of St Fillan, and second, the scene of the famous fight of

Bridge of Dochart

Dalry. Those who wish to visit these noteworthy points and to see the beauties of great Glen Lyon, should stop a day at Tyndrum, where they will find an exceptionally comfortable hotel. The reason for the presence of such a large and well appointed hotel at Tyndrum is that the place is in high favour with mountaineers as a centre and for anglers.

Strathfillan was one of the earliest routes in Scotland along which Christianity made its way; and St Fillan, one of the first preachers of the Gospel in the north, came down the glen, journeying from Iona, and established here a Culdee church, now known as St Fillan's Chapel. It lies on the left of the line, about two miles and a half from Crianlarich.

The old bell has been taken to Edinburgh, but a still more interesting reminder of the past is the Holy Pool. In this the sick used to be dipped to cure them of their troubles; and a still more curious method was adopted towards the mentally diseased. Lunatics used to be brought to the Pool, from far and near, bound hand and foot, and thrown in. At the bottom of the Pool there were a number of large pebbles and if the drowning wretch could bring up one of these, when he came to the surface, he was regarded as miraculously restored to sanity, and the pebble was added to a cairn on the bank as a memorial. If he failed to bring up the stone, even then the cure of the lunatic was not regarded as absolutely hopeless. He was given another chance — if such a one-sided ordeal can be called a chance for a poor demented creature. He was dragged out of the Pool, and laid on a certain place on the floor of the Chapel, still bound hand and foot. There he was left all night on a slab of stone, half drowned and helpless. If in the morning it was found that he had succeeded in loosing his bonds, then he was proclaimed sane — the devils that possessed him having been driven out by St Fillan; but if he was discovered in the morning still tied fast, then he was an incurable lunatic. If a person, already deficient in mental balance, were put through the experiences we have related, there would be little doubt, we should imagine, about his lunacy in the morning, if he survived. In this respect the treatment was doubtless successful, that it removed all dubiety, either bringing his madness to a head, or despatching him to his long home. Witches, too, used to be brought to this Holy Pool, and tested in an equally disagreeable way. Their thumbs and great toes were tied together, and they were cast into the water. If in this plight they succeeded in either floating or in scrambling ashore, they were proved witches, and were burned at the stake accordingly; but if they sank, and remained down, then they were innocent; and were probably found to be drowned when dragged out.

About two miles beyond St Fillan's Chapel, on the same side of the line, by the bank of the stream, is the scene of the Battle of Dalry — inseparably connected in the memory with the name of Robert the Bruce. Having slain his rival the Red Comyn, before the high altar of the Church of the Minorites, in Dumfries, he was compelled to raise his standard against Edward the First sooner than he had intended. He hastily collected his followers, and was crowned King of Scotland, in the Abbey of Scone, in March 1306; but in June was totally defeated near Methven, in Perthshire. With a few brave adherents, Bruce retreated into the Highlands, where great hardships were suffered, the little band being frequently attacked and driven from one place to another. When he attempted to penetrate into Argyllshire he found the M'Dougals in arms against him, under their chief, John of Lorn, who was a relative of the assassinated Red Comyn. The remainder of the tale may best be told in the words of Sir Walter Scott:– "Bruce was defeated by this chief, through force of numbers, at a place called Dalry; but he showed, amidst his misfortunes, the greatness of his strength and courage. He directed his men to retreat through a narrow pass, and placing himself last of the party, he fought with, and slew such of the enemy as attempted to press hard on them. Three followers of M'Dougal, a father and two sons, called M'Androsser, all very strong men, when they saw Bruce thus protecting the retreat of his followers, made a vow that they would either kill this redoubted champion or make him prisoner. The whole three rushed on the King at once. Bruce was on horseback, in the straight pass we have described, betwixt a precipitous rock and a deep lake. He struck the first man, who came up and seized his horse's rein, such a blow with his sword, as cut off his hand and freed the bridle. The man bled to death. The other brother had grasped Bruce in the meantime by the leg and was attempting to throw him from horseback. The King, setting spurs to his horse, made the animal suddenly spring forward, so that the Highlander fell under the horse's feet; and, as he was endeavouring to rise again, Bruce cleft his head in two with his sword. The father, seeing his two sons thus slain, flew desperately at the King, and grasped him by the mantle so close to his body, that he could not have room to wield his long sword. But with the heavy pommel of that weapon, or, as others say, with an iron hammer which hung at his saddle-bow, the King struck this third assailant so heavy a blow that he dashed out his brains. Still, however, the Highlander kept his dying grasp on the King's mantle; so that, to be free of the dead body, Bruce was obliged to undo his brooch, or clasp, by which it was fastened, and leave that, and the mantle itself, behind him. The brooch, which fell thus into the possession of M'Dougal of Lorn, is still preserved in that ancient family, as a memorial that the celebrated Robert Bruce once narrowly escaped falling into the hands of their ancestor."

About a mile beyond Dalry, Tyndrum Station is reached, four and a half miles from Crianlarich, and 41 from Craigendoran. On the hill to the left, above the hotel, there used to be lead-mines worked by Lord Breadalbane; they lie about two-thirds up the hill, and never paid owing to the cost of transport. All the hills in this neighbourhood are rich in lead, and may be opened up now that the railway runs to their base. About a mile beyond Tyndrum the line crosses the county march between Perthshire and Argyllshire, at an elevation of 1,025 feet. The boundary is the great watershed of Scotland, and we find the mountain torrents now pouring westward to the Atlantic through Argyllshire, instead of eastward through Perthshire to the German Ocean. The course of the line is along the slopes of wild hills, bare of trees, that would be dark and forbidding but for the warm glow of the heather that clothes their rocky sides, turning the barren wilderness into a blaze of colour. The great bulk of Ben Doran is seen in front, and presently we reach its very foot, after curving round a horse-shoe loop by two viaducts at Auch, which lies at the mouth of Glen Lyon. This is one of the grandest and one of the longest glens in Scotland, stretching right through to Aberfeldy. A coach-road is meditated from the railway to this glen, so that travellers may strike eastward if they wish. The route will be particularly attractive in conjunction with that we are now describing — from Craigendoran, the whole length of the West Highland line to Fort William, back by Ballachullish and Glencoe to Bridge of Orchy, and thence, with only a few miles over the track already followed, eastward through Glen Lyon to Aberfeldy.

The natural approach to the Glen is from Auch, the coach-road to follow the shores of Loch Lyon; but the necessities of construction makes the starting point Gortan, seven and a half miles north-east, as the crow flies, the coach-road passing down Glen Murran to Invermurran, at the foot of the Loch, where the actual Glen would be entered. Between the two routes there is little to choose in point of picturesqueness; but, for the pedestrian, the best approach at present is by way of Tyndrum and Auch.

The railway, on leaving Auch behind, passes round the side of Ben Doran, which towers up on the right to a height of 3,523 feet, in a fine steep slope, the close proximity of this grand mountain being one of the most impressive scenic features yet encountered by the traveller along this ever-varying route. It seems taking a most unwarrantable liberty

Re-assuring Swiss chalet style of Tyndrum Upper . . .

In marked contrast to bargain basement Tyndrum Lower

to cut a railway along the base of a mountain about which Ossian raved, and about which Duncan Ban McIntyre, the last of the great Gaelic bards, composed that grand song, like a march played on the bag-pipes, which Donald Malloch of Crianlarich, the descendant of Malachi the Prophet, can chant so well over a half-mutchkin! On the left the desolate hills of Glen Orchy are seen, branching off to the south-west, wild as a nightmare.

Glen Orchy leads down to the head of Loch Awe, and it is by that Loch that Glenstrae lies, and Coalchuirn (or Kilchurn) Castle. About seven miles and a half from Tyndrum the train reaches Bridge of Orchy.

At this point, some forty-eight and a half miles from Craigendoran, even the coach-road stopped, in the days before the railway was constructed, and travellers who wished to go further north had to trust to their own legs or to those of a hill pony, for the track was little more than a sheep-path.

Ever since leaving Crianlarich, some 12 miles back, we have been travelling through a country consecrated to sport, of which fact a significant illustration is to be seen in the little rattling squares of tin hung at intervals along the telegraph wires, and particularly at the openings of glens. These are known as 'grouse protectors', and are hung thus in order that their noise in the wind may warn the grouse of the existence of a danger, and prevent them hurling themselves in full flight against the telegraph wires.

But although those steep hill slopes, those sunken valleys, and those stretches of barren moorland, have been unbroken by human habitation, save an

Passing place at Bridge of Orchy in the days when 'real' trains still ran on the West Highland line

occasional lonely shieling, and have been peopled only by deer and wildfowl, and the coney that "maketh his dwelling amongst the rocks"; it is only now that we are entering the real home of the wild game, both great and small. For about five-and-twenty miles due north the land is untrodden, except by the sportsman and the shepherd. The last connection with the South breaks off at Bridge of Orchy, the coach-road striking away to the north-west towards Glencoe. Those who wish to see that sublime Glen will find a coach service from Bridge of Orchy, right through to Ballachulish on Loch Leven, whence a steamer will take them north to Fort William, to Inverness by the Caledonian Canal, or south to Oban, by Loch Linnhe. But the most interesting route is to proceed by the West Highland all the way to Fort William, and return through Glencoe to Bridge of Orchy, thus making a complete circuit, then going eastward by Glen Lyon, a route to be made shortly practicable by the construction of a coach-road. There is no hotel at Bridge of Orchy*, but it is a short run to Tyndrum, where an excellent hotel will be found.

On leaving Bridge of Orchy, the railway follows for a mile and a half the course of the River Orchy, which lies a quarter of a mile to the left. On the moor between the river and the railway, will be observed a gigantic boulder, weighing some thousands of tons. This is Rob Roy's

Rob Roy's Putting Stone
Glen orchy

* *Today, of course, Bridge of Orchy has a fine hotel.*

Putting Stone", which the mighty MacGregor endeavoured to 'put' from the top of Ben Doran across the valley to the hill opposite. For the literal accuracy of this anecdote we do not vouch: we give it as we got it from a simple-hearted native, who was anxious to give us the fullest information about the district.

Presently the river is lost in Loch Tulla, a sheet of water about two and a half miles long by three quarters wide, noted for its salmon and trout fishing. The line runs along the Loch side, but at a considerable height above the water, and a fine view is obtained of the great Black Mount deer forest, which the railway skirts for about ten miles. It covers an area of 80,000 acres, stretching as far west as Glen Etive and Glencoe, and is one of the best in Scotland. It belongs to the Marquis of Breadalbane, whose shooting lodge may be seen among the trees on the south-western shore of the Loch. To those unfamiliar with Scotland it will appear to be a misnomer to call this vast area of barren mountains and waste moorlands a deer forest, for on it, except in a few isolated patches, there seems to grow nothing higher than heather; but, nevertheless, it is a model of what a Scottish deer forest should be.

From the north-eastern extremity of the Loch the Water of Tulla finds exit, the railway continuing to follow the course of the valley. About a mile beyond the Loch, on the bank of the Tulla Water, lies a picturesque old ruin, Achallader Castle, an ancient stronghold of the Fletchers. Around this lonely keep many a tough fight was fought some centuries ago, and the graves of the slain are marked by cairns and on the neighbouring heath. Soon after this ruin is passed the line enters the Crannach Wood, another relic of the great Caledonian Forest. The wood covers a tract about a mile square, beginning on the eastern bank of the Tulla Water and extending up the hillside, so that it lies both to right and left of the railway. Like the former remnants of the Caledonian Forest we saw in Glen Falloch, the trees are grand and aged types of the real Scottish fir, their great red and grey trunks bent "in a thousand shapes of resistance and of destruction, their knotted and tortuous branches stretched out in sturdy and fantastic forms of defiance to the whirlwind and the winter." They are thinly scattered over the muir and up the hill, the shadow of one hardly reaching to the foot of another, but to look along a vista of such trees as those, the sombre green of their wide-spread branches standing out in strong relief against the background of purple heather and brown mosses on the hillside, is an experience never forgotten by the artistic mind. It is a picture the composition of which has taken many a century of that infinite care which Nature bestows upon her work.

Crannach Wood, near Gortan

AS WE emerge from the old Caledonian Forest, we get the first glimpse of Ben Nevis, rearing its snow-clad peak twenty miles to the north-west, but the hills on either hand gradually recede, and instead of threading a narrow glen, we find ourselves traversing an undulating moorland, ever widening and increasing in grandeur. We are entering on the third great section of the journey. During the first, the vast Lochs were all in all; along the second, the majesty of the mountains overshadowed us; and now comes a striking change, in the shape of the famous Moor of Rannoch.

About a mile beyond the Crannach Wood is a passing place called Gortan, whence, according to one scheme, the coach-road for Glen Lyon will diverge to the right, as already explained. The flat country between the Caldedonian Forest and Gortan, is called the Crannach Moor, and is not, strictly speaking, part of the great desert we have now to cross; but at Gortan the Moor of Rannoch may be said to begin.

Rannoch Moor is the great table-land of Scotland, and even the Moor of Caithness shrinks into insignificance beside it. It is about twenty miles

Tree roots in the peat on Rannoch Moor

square, and is surrounded by an amphitheatre of hills, seen dimly in the distance. To say that it is a morass, twenty miles long and twenty miles broad, would convey a mental picture suggesting the most dismal reflections to the traveller who has booked through. We, therefore, hasten to reassure him by asserting emphatically that the Moor of Rannoch is one of the most picturesque stretches on the whole route, and is better described as a wide expanse of moorland, broken up by a multitude of little hillocks and big granite boulders, with peaty tarns and diminutive lochs in the hollows.

When an artist, on a sketching tour, reaches the Moor of Rannoch, there he remains until his time is exhausted. Monotonous it certainly is to the pedestrian, who toils over it heavy-footed from Kinloch Rannoch to Kingshouse; but from the window of a railway-carriage it is the reverse of wearisome. There is an infinite solitude in its vast and open expanse, that renders it a spectacle never to be erased from the memory of the dweller in busy cities. An idea of its loneliness and weird uniformity, may, perhaps, best be conveyed by mentioning the fact that in winter it has been no uncommon thing for shepherds to be lost in the snow, and to perish on the Moor for lack of landmarks — those hardy Highland shepherds who know every stone, every bush, every tuft of heather almost, on the miles over which their flocks winter. Macculloch has described the moor as "a great level, 1,000 feet above the sea, sixteen or twenty miles long, and nearly as much wide, bounded by mountains so distant as scarcely to form an appreciable boundary — open, silent, solitary. Not even the mountain bee was on the wing to give life to the scene; nay, the very midges seemed to scorn the Moor of Rannoch. No water stirred to indicate that something yet lived or moved. The heart-sinking stillness of this solitude was the more dreary that it was so spacious."

This is a very vivid piece of word-painting, from the point of view of a man on foot; but he was unfortunate in the season of his visit as regards insect-life. Why, the whole moor in summer is a-buzz with bees; there are midges in plenty, if they can be taken as any amelioration of the dreariness of the waste, and there are burns where the dark brown dappled beauty of the burn trout is well known to the skilful angler. Moreover, it is, perhaps, the finest grouse-moor in Scotland, and it is over-run, particularly towards the hills, with the white hare. During the construction of the railway, a party of five guns in a day's shooting bagged 150 hares, an average of 30 to the gun. Among those who have not seen the moor, the impression is that it is as flat as the face of a loch, but this is by no means so. It is full of undulations and little knolls, and it is the complete absence of tree and shrub that invests it with such utter nakedness. The surface is the most treacherous walking imaginable, the bog being broken throughout into tufts of sod, separated by peat "hags" — shallow black ditches, meandering hither and thither, and forming a maze of slippery snares for the pedestrian, at every few yards. In winter the moor is simply twenty miles square of a study in sepia; but in summer the brilliance of the colouring is marvellous. The purple heather, the green mosses, the yellow grasses, and the rich brown of the peat hags, with here and there the delicate azure of the harebell — by itself, all but unseen — combine to form a luminous mass of lovely tints. The whole moor appears to be covered with one colossal Turkey carpet, so rich and oriental is the colouring.

All around in the peat hags, projecting from the sides of the rent moss, are to be seen the brown contorted roots of enormous trees, with here and there a splintered section of a huge trunk, giving unmistakeable evidence that this unclad waste was once covered by a mighty race of trees, the ancient Caledonian Forest, whose survivors we have seen. Wherever a cutting is made on Rannoch Moor, there roots and stumps of giant firs are found; and it is curious to learn, that although the wood may have been buried in the soaking moss for a thousand years, it burns like a torch. Not only has the bed of peat preserved it from decay, but the old pine roots retain their resin and oils. It is not very many years since these ancient roots were the favourite means of illumination in the shielings of the district. We know of an old shepherd and his wife who used to live in a hut towards Kingshouse, on the western verge of Rannoch Moor, who unwillingly abandoned the use of this primitive lamp in favour of paraffin only some few years ago. When he had gathered his flock into the fold, the shepherd would return to his low thatch-covered shieling with an armful of the roots, to be dried before the great peat fire for a night. In the morning he would break them into small pieces, about the size of a finger, and in the dark winter evenings it was the duty of the old man to keep one of the little torches flaring while his aged wife sat spinning at her wheel in the ingle-neuk.

The method of burning the roots was curious. From the crook in the chimney hung an iron instrument, like the 'girdle' on which oat-cakes are baked, but instead of presenting to the fire a flat surface, the 'girdle' was ribbed with bars like a gridiron. One of the small pieces of resinous fir-root was placed on these bars and blazed up in the heat of the fire, illuminating the whole hut, and as soon as the flare began to die out the old shepherd would put on another, the whirr of the spinning-wheel never ceasing. Such a spectacle as this was to be seen until quite recently in hundreds of shielings around the moor.

Even if the traveller be inclined to regard the Moor of Rannoch as dismal, the landscape will assume a new interest in his eyes when he is reminded that it is the scene of some of the most exciting episodes in that heart-stirring book of Robert Louis Stevenson's *Kidnapped*, one of the finest pieces of word-painting, and character sketching, published since the death of Scott.

At Gortan, we enter Rannoch Moor, and proceed through the midst of that silent waste, which stretches for miles and miles to the right and left, until its dazzling colours die into the brown distance, and at last merge in the blue of the far-away hills surrounding the desert. To travel over this section by day is a memorable experience, but best of all it is to cross the moor in the evening, for the sunsets on that desolate moss are incredibly beautiful. As the sun sinks behind the distant western peaks it turns them to gold, while their shoulders darken into a profound blue, like the blue of mid-ocean, and the level rays of the dying orb pour over the vast plain in broad pathways of light, shedding a new glory on the sodden moss and turning the dark peat-hags into streaks of silver, around which the heather and clusters of wild flowers spring up like flames of fire. The sun dips behind the mountain-tops leaving only a radiance in the sky, and a grey veil seems to descend on the moor, fold by fold, dimming the bright hues of the barren heath until all around lies a dreary brown expanse, like the Sargasso Sea, tossing its matted weed in hillocks after a storm; while on the west, some distant glen lies, like a Land of Goshen, in a very noontide of sunlight. Those who wish to know this wonderful moor, as it should be known, must so time their journeys that either the first visit or the return is in the evening. To see a sunset on Rannoch Moor is as essential as to see Loch Lomond by moonlight.

Rannoch Moor used to be regarded as an impassable barrier by railway engineers. Several

Steam returns – briefly – to Bridge of Or chy as Black Five 5407 (along with NB 673 'Maude') pauses en r oute for Fort William and service on the Mallaig line

schemes were mooted in the past, but they always broke down at Rannoch Moor. As now constructed, the West Highland Railway virtually floats over the moor. The moor was deep and cross-drained to take off the water, and across the trenches was laid a thick layer of brushwood. On this elastic foundation the permanent way was laid, making one of the most satisfactory stretches on the line. Instead of the brushwood decaying in the wet peat, as one might be inclined to think, it is pickled and preserved like the roots of the old pine trees which we have described. Maybe a thousand years hence, if excavations are made, the brushwood will be found as fresh as the day it was deposited. There is no question that the line has been well engineered. When Mr Charles Forman, whose scheme it is, had laid down his route from Craigendoran, to Fort William, he was astonished to discover in some old Parliamentary papers that an almost identical course, for a turnpike road, had been traced in the beginning of the century by Telford, the famous engineer who constructed the Caldedonian Canal. In one sense it was a curious coincidence, but more properly it might be said to be a voucher for the soundness of the plan, since two engineers had arrived independently at the same conclusions at different dates.

Near Gortan, the county march, between Argyllshire and Perthshire, is again crossed, and for a few miles the railway runs in the latter county again. The watershed is once more traversed, and the streams are now found flowing east to the German Ocean. The Tulla Water on the left is followed for some way, and then the Blackwater is

Maude, in light steam, pauses at Bridge of Orchy before, below, setting off for the journey across the Moor of Rannoch

taken up on the same side — both narrow streams winding through the irregular surface of the moor. Near the bridge over the Blackwater are seen, on both sides of the line, the 'Sodiers' Trenches', long parallels cut through the moss and rapidly filling up with the spongy peat. These are a relic of the '45 , having been cut by the Duke of Cumberland's men after the Jacobite rising. A body of English troops was posted at Rannoch, where the barracks are still to be seen near the Loch, to keep the Highlanders of the district in order. Finding time hanging heavily on the men's hands, their commander set them to the task of digging these trenches, which were absolutely useless for any defensive purpose, as they could be turned on either flank, lying as they did right in the middle of the waste.

The railway, which has made a bend to the east, now runs north to the Gauer Water, a swift stream flowing between Loch Lydoch on the left and Loch Rannoch on the right; crossing the stream a mile east of the foot of Loch Lydoch, and reaching Rannoch Station, fifteen and a half miles from Bridge of Orchy. Rannoch cannot well claim to be populous*, although at the head of Loch Rannoch, seven miles away, there are a number of houses, and along its sides there is a considerable crofting population. Kinloch Rannoch, on the eastern end of the Loch, is a favourite summer resort, notwithstanding the difficulties of its approach which have had hitherto to be encountered. There is a geographical amenity about the place, however, for it is to be the starting point of a coach road along the Gauer and the north side of Loch Rannoch to Struan on the Highland Railway, thus making a very

* *Today there is an excellent hotel near the station.*

Rannoch station and welcoming platfor m tea room – one lump or two?

useful connection for the traveller to the Braemar Highlands and the northern counties.

Gauer Water, Schehallion in the distance

On leaving Rannoch we have a fine view along Loch Lydoch, a narrow sheet of water about five miles long, inclining to the south-west, the brilliant blue of its waters making a beautiful picture amid the surrounding bloom of the heather. The railway now makes a sharp bend to the north-west and skirts Cruach Hill, from which point, owing to the high elevation and the open view, one of the most magnificent prospects on the whole route is obtained. On the left, Loch Lydoch extends into the heart of the Black Mount, where the great hills rise in bold and precipitous crags, looming dark against

Flower beds and a smartly painted footbridge at Rannoch, starting point for one of the bleak est parts of the line, accessed by a fine lattice girder viaduct to the north of the station.

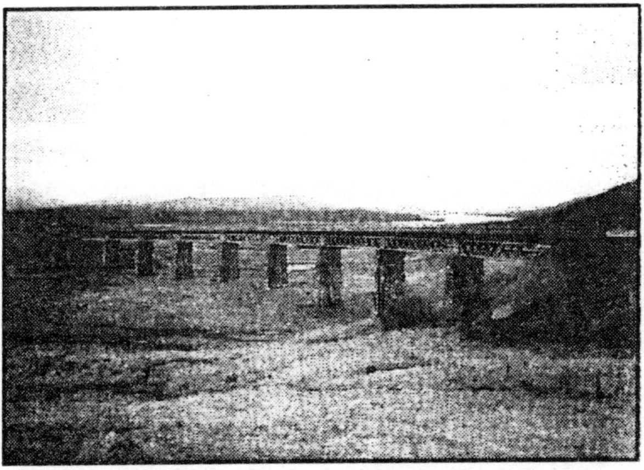

the sky, while further west, tower the mountains of Glen Etive and Glencoe — a mightly and turbulent sea of hills. Far away, in the north-west, are clustered the peaks of Lochaber, with the huge summit of Ben Nevis soaring over all. On the right, to the south-east, are grouped the gloomy mountains of Glen Lyon; further east may be descried, in the distance, the huge bulk of Schehallion, and north-east opens Glen Ericht, looked down upon by great Ben Alder. In whichever direction the eye be cast it is confronted by a colossal barrier of rock, heaving up into the sky in a thousand impressive outlines.

Towards Ben Alder the traveller will turn with peculiar interest, for it was on that 'wild desert mountain, full of hills and hollows', which rises to a height of 3,757 feet, that the heroes of *Kidnapped* found safety on their escape from the moor. On the southern flank of 'that dismal mountain of Ben Alder' lies what is known as 'Prince Charlie's Cave', where the Young Pretender lay hid with Cluny Macpherson and Lochiel, after the disastrous battle of Culloden. This was one of the refuges in which Cluny, the Chief of the Clan Macpherson, lived for about nine years after that battle, safe in the fidelity of his people, although his country was over-run by troops who would have gone to any pains to capture this Jacobite leader, had they known of his proximity. Under the name of 'Cluny's Cage', a very good description of this curious lair is given by Stevenson, when Alan Breck and David Balfour seek asylum there with Cluny Macpherson: "We came at last to the foot of an exceeding steep wood, which scrambled up a craggy hillside, and was crowned by a naked precipice. The trees clung upon the slope, like sailors on the shrouds of a ship; and their trunks were like the rounds of a ladder, by which we mounted. Quite at the top, and just before the rocky face of the cliff sprang above the foliage, we found that strange house, which was known in the country as 'Cluny's Cage'. The trunks of several trees had been wattled across, the intervals strengthened with stakes, and the ground behind this barricade levelled up with earth to make the floor. A tree, which grew out from the hillside, was the living centrebeam of the roof. The walls were of wattle and covered with moss. The whole house had something of an egg-shape; and it half hung, half stood, in that steep, hillside thicket, like a wasp's nest in a green hawthorn. Within, it was large enough to shelter five or six persons with some comfort. A projection of the cliff had been cunningly employed to be the fireplace, and the smoke rising against the face of the rock, and being not dissimilar in colour, readily escaped notice from below."

South of Ben Alder lies Loch Ericht, which Christopher North describes as "the dreariest, most desolate, and dismal of the Highland Lochs," and the distance from the West Highland Railway, up Glen Ericht to Dalwhinnie, on the Highland Railway, is seventeen and a half miles, this being the nearest point of approach between the two railways.

Skirting, on the left, the rocky eminences known as the Black Corries, the line passes close on the same side, a tarn called Loch-na-Chlaidheimh, which is a point of considerable interest. The name is pronounced Loch-na-Clive, the last syllable being apparently unnecessary, but Gaelic is a peculiar language; for instance, what we pronounce Ben Venue is written in Gaelic, Beinn Mheadhonaidh. The Loch is the most easterly of a chain of small lakes, joined first by the Blackwater (not the stream of the same name we crossed before) and afterwards by the River Leven, which stretch from east to west, to the head of Loch Leven — an arm of Loch Linnhe. In the centre of Loch-na-Chlaidheimh three counties meet — Inverness-shire, Perthshire and Argyllshire, and thereby hangs a tale.

The name means 'the Loch of the Swords', and the story is this — Late in the fifteenth century, Lochiel, the Chief of the Camerons, and the Earl of Atholl, the head of the Atholl family, agreed to meet alone by this Loch and settle certain boundary disputes. As Lochiel was on his way to the place of appointment, he was met by an old woman, who stopped the Chief on the moor with the significant question, "Where are your men, Lochiel?" The Chief laughed, but the old woman kept her blear eyes fixed steadily on his face, and croaked out again, "Where are your men, Lochiel?" "Peace, old witch!" said Lochiel; "what need have I of a following? I go to meet only Atholl," and he strode off. But the uncanny old woman hobbled after him, caught him by the streaming end of his cloak, and muttered again, with strange persistence, "Where are your men, Lochiel?" The Chief could not help feeling uneasy at this obstinate prediction of evil, and gave way, returning to the nearest clachan and collecting a 'tail' of sixty-five men, who followed him stealthily and secreted themselves among the heather by the loch-side. Presently the Earl of Atholl was seen approaching alone, and Lochiel felt

Cruachan snow shed, showing cor rugated iron roof and, below, southern entrance.

ashamed of his ambush. The two Chiefs met, and soon came to high words, whereupon the Earl waved his hand and twenty Atholl Highlanders sprang up from the heather, where they had been posted in advance. "Who are these?" said Lochiel. "Atholl wethers," replied the Earl, significantly, "come to graze on Lochaber pastures." Lochiel had arranged that if he turned his cloak so as to present the red side outwards, it was a signal for his men to show themselves; this he now did, and instantly his three score and five warriors came bounding down the grassy steep. Atholl started, and "Who are these?" said he. "Lochaber dogs," replied Lochiel, "sharp toothed and hungry, and, oh! so keen to taste the flesh of your Atholl wethers. Give up, Lord Earl, your claim to these lands, for my dogs are fierce and cannot much longer be held in leash." Peaceful negotiations then ensued, and the Earl of Atholl, drawing his sword and kissing it, renounced his claim "through summer's heat and winter's cold"; and sweeping his sword round his head, tossed it into the lake, proclaiming that the land should be Lochiel's till the sword was found.

Singularly enough, in 1826, a boy fishing in the Loch, brought a basket-hilted sword to land, and took it to the minister of the parish, but so alarmed were the Lochaber men on hearing the discovery that they demanded its restoration, and it was again thrown into the Loch.

At the 'Sword Loch' the railway enters Inverness-shire, in which county it remains until the terminus at Fort William is reached. To the north-west of the bare little Loch rises the commanding eminence of Ben-na-Vreich, jutting out as the sharp separation of two valleys. On the left of the railway the Blackwater valley stretches due west to Loch Leven, while on the right the valley of the Tay opens eastward, with proud Schehallion in the distance. A little further on, to the left, about two and a half miles distant to the north-east, a large house is seen, across the moor, and half way up the hill. This is Corrour Lodge, the highest shooting lodge in Scotland, being 1,723 feet above the sea level. It is the property of Sir John Stirling Maxwell, of Pollock; and, according to the omniscient Baddeley, "it disputes with the 'Cat and Fiddle' near Buxton, the claim to the highest position of any habitation in the kingdom". It lies in the deer forest of Corrour, which we follow on the right, the forest of Ben-na-Vreich lying on the left. About three miles beyond Corrour Lodge, Loch Ossian is passed, a lonely tarn

Loch Ossian

Interior of the Cruachan snow shed

about four miles long, noted for its splendid trout, and is the highest Loch of any size in Scotland, its elevation above the sea level being 1,269 feet. Opposite this Loch is the passing place of Luibruiaridh (pronounced Lebruary), which is at once the termination of Rannoch Moor and the highest point on the line, being 1,350 feet above the sea. A fine view may be obtained, from this point, of Ben Nevis, which lies about twelve miles to the north-west, towering above the hills around it as the dome of St Paul's towers above the highest roofs of London.

On towards the snow covered peaks from remote Corrour.

RANNOCH MOOR is now left behind, and a new phase of scenery develops as the line, which has been running north-west from Rannoch to Corrour, strikes due north, and begins to descend into the Spean Valley. Christopher North, whose vigorous remarks on Highland scenery we have frequently quoted, speaks of a prodigious wilderness, with which perhaps no man alive is conversant, and in which you may travel for days without seeing even any symptoms of human life — the regions comprehended between the Forest of Atholl and Ben Nevis, the Moor of Rannoch and Glen Spean. There are many lochs, and Loch Ericht is their griesly Queen. Herdsmen, shepherds, hunters, fowlers, anglers, traverse its borders, but few have been far in the interior, and we never knew anybody who had crossed it from south to north, from east to west." Now, the West Highland Railway traverses it from south to north and from east to west, and the most frail invalid may inspect, at his ease, this prodigious wilderness, which even the Professor, with his mighty and untiring stride, never covered. But the association in one sentence of Rannoch Moor and Glen Spean must not mislead the reader of the *Recreations of Christopher North* into the idea that the two stretches of country are similar in aspect. They are totally distinct; the barren moorland is left behind at Luibruaridh and succeeded by a rugged and romantic country, possessing some of the most picturesque features on the whole hundred-mile run.

Soon after leaving Luibruaridh, Loch Treig comes into view on the left, lying within a stone's throw of

Loch Treig, looking towards Inverlair

the line, but 415 feet below, the railway being cut high in the hillside that overshadows it. Loch Treig is a most striking sheet of water, about five miles and a half in length, and about half a mile in width (at the head) which is first seen from the railway and gradually narrowing to the foot, while the line, winding down the shoulder of the hill on a steep gradient, finishes almost level with the water. On both sides of the Loch precipitous hills rise sheer from the lake, the banks being shelving rock. Some years ago, a boat containing two Highlanders capsized at the edge of the Loch, and one of the men was drowned. When the survivor was asked to explain how it happened he made the following perspicuous statement: "Well, sir, you will see, when the boat did turn over, Tonald and me went down into the water. Loch Treig, as you will know, is a very steep loch, and she herself will have taken the right turning and will have climbed out of the water; but Tonald will have taken the wrong turning and climbed down and been trownded."

Loch Treig is famous for its trout, the fish ranging as high as nine pounds, while twenty pounds is spoken of in the district as a fair day's basket. As the line dips to the foot of the Loch, a tiny islet is descried, bearing a few trees. This is "Council Island," where the chiefs of the Clan Cameron, and the Clan MacIntosh, used to confer when disputes arose between the two clans, and it was a question of peace or war. This little island was selected as the place of meeting in order that the two chiefs might be safe from such treacherous ambushes on either side as we described at the 'Sword Loch'. It had the additional advantage of being small and in deep water, so that if the two chiefs failed to come to an agreement, one of them was likely to go over, and the dispute thus be settled by the silence of one party, and the feud started on a satisfactory basis. On the hillside, overhanging the line, is a huge boulder called the 'Watch-Rock', on

Corrour, highest and most remote station on the line.

which the Highland sentinels used to stand to survey the surrounding country when the inroad of a rival clan was expected.

From the foot of Loch Treig pours the river Treig, gradually narrowing as it approaches the Spean, which it enters at Inverlair, after a furious passage down the moorland slopes in a series of foaming rapids. At Inverlair * there is a station of the West Highland Railway, seventeen miles from Rannoch, and about eighty-one from Craigendoran. From this point a coach-road strikes off to the north-east, through the Laggan district, along Spean-side and Loch Laggan, to Kingussie (pronounced King-yewsie), on the Highland Railway, whence the Braemar and Aberdeenshire Highlands may be reached.

At Inverlair, the West Highland Railway changes its course. Hitherto, although with various bends to the east or west, neccessitated by the nature of the country (for it is a land in which the towns will have to come to the railway, as there are no towns to which the railway can go), has been making due north, for the difference of longitude between Craigendoran and Inverlair is very minute.

But now the railway turns due west, crossing the Spean and following its course along the Glen on the northern bank, penetrating the famous Braes of Lochaber.

From Loch Laggan the river Spean pours in a swift torrent, carrying a very heavy volume of water compressed within a narrow channel, which it has cut for itself deep in the hard schist. The railway follows closely the north bank of the ravine down which the fierce current tears its way, the train

* *Now known as Tulloch.*

sometimes appearing to overhang the turbulent stream. The river is a succession of furious cataracts, one of the most striking being seen just after leaving Inverlair. The water thunders down a series of wide steps against a wall of rock so adamantine that the stream swerves at a sharp angle and rushes in a long race of white spume through a straight chute, cut in the black rock as if with the chisel. A little further and we pass, on the right, a village called Achluachrach (a striking name for a Cockney suburban villa), where there is an interesting old burying-ground called St Cyril. About this ancient God's Acre a quaint anecdote is told by the late Mrs MacKellar. "Once upon a time a Protestant was buried in this consecrated ground, and forthwith there was a rebellion among the dwellers in those tombs. Night after night the inhabitants of the surrounding districts were disturbed with the shouts of warriors engaged in battle, and the clashing of weapons. At last it came to be unendurable, and a deputation waited on Dr Ross, the minister of the parish, saying, even though this parishioner of his had been a good man and a friend to the district, yet that he must be removed, or else the dead would never sleep in peace. 'I am not going to remove him; why don't they turn him out when they're at it? said Dr Ross; 'if he had twenty of his own kind with him they would clear the whole churchyard.' The matter, however, came to a crisis on a very stormy night. Women and children sat by the fire in their huts, cowering in fear. One good man at last resolved to venture out and go for the priest, which he did. The priest readily agreed to accompany him, and at a stream

After Tulloch station, above, the line runs through woods and hills towards Spean Bridge – and the sea.

he put off a shoe and prepared some holy water in it, with which he proceeded alone to where the Braes men, fierce and furious, were in vain endeavouring to oust this disturber of their rest." The moment the priest had reconsecrated the ground the tumult ceased, and it was never afterwards renewed.

On the hills to the right there has been visible, from Inverlair to this point, one of the mysterious Parallel Roads of Lochaber, which were for so many years a source of sore perplexity among men of science. Of these strange Parallel Roads we shall have more to say when we reach Glen Roy, where the most wonderful examples are found. As we advance along the Spean the valley narrows until it becomes little more than a ravine, and at Monessie Gorge the waterfalls are striking in the extreme. The gorge is narrow and deep, dark crags, fringed with trees, shutting in the rushing torrent, which seethes in thunder and foam down the steep and rocky channel, leaping over the obstructing boulders in clouds of spray that beat on the carriage windows when the stream is in spate, for the train runs on the absolute verge of the cataract, separated from the roaring current only by a low parapet. No obstacle on the line more forcibly impresses the memory than these Monessie Falls, the steep black rocks, the dark green foliage at the waters edge, and the white torrent boiling down the rugged bed in a mad delirious ferment, forming a picture that seems an embodiment of the spirit of the Highlands, proud, turbulent and untameable.

A little beyond Monessie, the train stops at Roy Bridge station, about five miles and a half from

Inverlair. Here the railway crosses the River Roy, which comes down from Glen Roy, where the Parallel Roads are to be seen. No one should visit this district without inspecting these geological wonders, either by making a trip to the Glen from Fort William, about twelve miles distant, or breaking the journey for the purpose at Roy Bridge, where a hotel will be found. On a clear day a glimpse of the Roads may be had from the train; but to study these natural phenomena it is necessary to walk or drive a few miles up the Glen.

Parallel Roads of Glen Roy

These Parallel roads have caused one of the keenest scientific controversies of the century, and although their mystery is now solved, they are still regarded as one of the most unique features in the geological aspect of the country; while even to the non-scientific observer they are full of strange interest. Glen Roy is a gloomy ravine, both long and deep, but less than half a mile wide, shut in on both sides by steep mountain slopes, along whose bases the valley winds its way. Standing at the mouth of the Glen, the observer is amazed to see three distinct horizontal lines running along the eastern hillsides — exactly parallel — the two upper lines far up the hills and separated by about eighty feet, while the lower lies about 200 feet further down the slope. On looking to the western hillsides, he is still more startled to see three exactly similar lines running along the Glen on that side also, not only parallel to each other, but parallel to those on the east, and at precisely the same elevations, the lines following each other for about eight miles. "The long, deep Glen lies before him, with its three bars, straight and distinct, as if they had been drawn with a ruler, yet winding into all the recesses of the steep slopes, and coming out again, over the projecting parts, without ever deviating from their parallelism." His astonishment is increased when, on close inspection, he finds that each of these lines is a level terrace, cut in the face of the hills, and ranging in places over sixty feet in width. How these terraces were cut used to be a problem puzzled over as much by the scientist as by the layman. The Highlanders said they were hunting-walks cut by the Picts for their kings, who used to hold court in Inverlochy Castle, beside Fort William; but this was obviously absurd. The pseudo-scientific visitor said the Roads must have been cut by glaciers at different periods, although they do not show the slightest evidence of

Above: incongruous fifties brutalism at Spean Bridge. The attractive Swiss chalet style station, below, has been given new life as a line-side restaurant.

glacial action. The truth, as at last discovered, is, that the terraces mark the successive levels of a great loch, "The shores, as it were, of a phantom lake, that came into being with the growth of the glaciers, and vanished as these melted away." That this wide-mouthed glen, opening into another glen, the valley of the Spean, should have been filled with a lake in days gone by seems incredible, but so it was.

At Roy Bridge, on the left, is Keppoch House, the ancient seat of the MacDonells of Keppoch. This was the scene of the 'Keppoch Murder', so terribly avenged, which took place in 1663. The chieftain of the MacDonells of Keppoch had died, leaving two young sons, who were being educated in France. On their father's death the lads came home, and invited their uncle's seven sons to dine with them. These surly youths, jealous of the succession to power of their two cousins, picked a quarrel with them over their French manners, slew them with their dirks, and seized the inheritance. Old Ian Lom, the Keppoch bard, on disovering what had happened, set out north for Invergarry, on the bank of Loch Oich, through which the Caledonian Canal now runs. Having reached the Castle he demanded of Lord Macdonnell and Aross, the chief of the clan, revenge against the murderers of his kinsmen. The chief gave him fifty men, with whom the bard returned to Keppoch, seized the house, slew the seven brothers, and cut off their heads. He then set out again for Invergarry, carrying the heads on his back, bound together by a heather-rope through their hair. "He went with them, glad as a farmer carrying golden sheaves, and laid them down at the feet of

Glengarry, after washing them in the well of the seven heads that stands on the banks of Loch Oich." The name of this well is Tober-na'n-Ceann, which means 'the well of the heads'. Over the well there is now a monument, surmounted by seven heads in stone.

Opposite Keppoch House, on the north side of the railway, rises an eminence of 800 feet called Mullroy (in Gaelic: *Maol Ruadh*), the hill on which the last clan-battle was fought in Scotland.

The famous Parallel Roads of Glen Roy are reached from here. Keppoch is passed on the left. The residence of its ancient Kings was an island on the Spean. But the river has now changed its course. The garden famous for its pears was destroyed by Cumberland after the '45. Here Viscount Dundee held a council of the Jacobite Chiefs in 1689, and marched at the head of a large band of warriors to gain a brilliant victory for King James at Killiecrankie, where a silver bullet was said to have ended the mortal career of 'Bonnie Dundee'.

'Inch' was the home of Colonel Archibald Macdonell, of the 92nd Highlanders, who served with that distinguished corps through the Peninsular War. Two cairns which we passed under St Cyril's, were raised to commemorate his son Ewen, who signalised himself during the Indian Mutiny, and his grandson Alister.

'Tirindrish', on the right, gave its name to the gallant and intrepid Major Donald Macdonald of the '45. He had the honour of firing the first shot for Prince Charlie in the rising of that year. On the 19th August, Major Macdonald, at Highbridge, lower down on the Spean, with a small party of men attacked and took prisoner Captain Scott, of the 1st Regiment of Foot, on his way with a detachment from Fort Augustus to strengthen the garrison at Fort William. Captain Scott was severely wounded, and Major Macdonald sent to the Governor of Fort William for medical aid, which was refused. The generous captor then had his prisoner conveyed to Tirindrish, where every care was bestowed on him and he was, after recovery, released on parole, which he faithfully observed. Captain (afterwards General) Scott left an immense fortune to his daughters, the Duchess of Portland and Lady Canning. In after years he met Major Macdonald's daughter at a Bath assembly, and feelingly described to her how he owed his life to her father's magnanimity, a striking contrast to the conduct of Cumberland's officers and men. Tirindrish was taken prisoner after the battle of Falkirk, with Sir Archibald Primrose, Kinloch, and others, sent to Carlisle, there barbarously despatched, and his head placed on the Scottish Gate, where it remained for many years. His speech on the scaffold, and farewell letters to his friends, give a fine impression of the nobility of his character. In later years Tirindrish was the residence of the Generals Ross.

At 'Auchendaul' lived another Peninsular veteran, Colonel Mitchell, of the 92nd, who took command of the regiment at Quartre Bras, when Colonel Cameron fell on the 16th June, 1815. He was wounded on that day, and at Waterloo the command of the 'gallant Gordons' devolved on Major Macdonald of Dalchosnie, who had the honour of leading them in the celebrated charge, at three o'clock, to face tremendous odds, which is said to have elicited from Napoleon the exclamation, "Les braves Ecossais". The later incident in this charge, the onslaught of the 'Scots Greys', is immortalised in Lady Butler's well-known picture, 'Scotland for ever". These words were uttered by each of these gallant corps as they passed each other, and in memory of that moment they have ever since dubbed themselves 'cousins'. Major Macdonald figures in James Grant's *Romance of War.*

After passing Keppoch House and Mullroy, a number of little cairns are seen on a heath to the right. These are 'resting-cairns' — memorials of the dead — and the importance of the deceased may be gauged by their size. The coffin is carried to the grave in these districts by the relatives and friends, and as the burying-ground is frequently a long way off, the body has to be set down at intervals in order that the bearers may rest. Whenever one of these pauses takes place, each of the mourners gathers a stone, and these stones are all piled up in a 'resting-cairn'. By counting the stones in one of the heaps the extent of the funeral procession could, therefore, be accurately arrived at. Near these cairns, the line passes through Inver-roy, a picturesque specimen of an old Highland clachan, unspoiled by modern improvements, the white shielings — low thatched huts — scattered at all angles, with the blue peat smoke pouring from their wooden chimneys, while bare-footed and bare-headed bairns toddle about on the brae-side, shouting to each other in Gaelic. The

Resting-cairns, Roy Bridge

line next crosses the Spean on a three-span bridge. It will interest the traveller who looks down from this bridge on the rapid Spean in summer, to know that in time of spate the water rises nearly twenty feet — to within a few feet of the girders.

The railway now follows the south bank of the Spean until Spean Bridge station is reached (three miles from Roy Bridge), where the river strikes off to the north-west to join the River Lochy, the combined waters flowing south-west and entering Loch Linnhe at Fort William.

At Spean Bridge there is a good hotel, with coach communication to Fort Augustus, the bridge being in the midst of a large pastoral district, while it is also within easy distance of the Caledonian Canal. We are now only some nine miles from Fort William, and are in the very midst of the Lochaber mountains, which are ranged to the south in stupendous groups: Ben Nevis surmounting all, although several of its neighbours are over 4,000 feet in height.

All along the glen, from Inverlair, we have been following the course of the romantic Spean, while to the south the vast congregation of mountains has been gradually opening out, glowing in all the colours of the rainbow according to the variations of light and shade; for, bare as a Highland Ben may seem at first sight, it is marvellously tinted, and its many hues melt and change, like the plumage of the 'burnished dove', with every new level of the sun's rays and every new change of atmosphere. From Spean Bridge we draw nearer and nearer to Ben Nevis and his brethren, but we lose the river, which disappears to the right down a birch and oak-clad

Following closure of the disastrous Fort Augustus branch back in 1933 a bus service bravely ran for some years. Below: the London sleeper under threat from the regulator

glen. A short distance along this glen lies High Bridge, one of General Wade's famous viaducts, built when he made one of his military roads from Fort William. It was here that the Jacobites, in the '45, had their first skirmish with King George's troops, a party of soldiers marching from Fort Augustus to Fort William having been surprised here by a large body of the Clan Cameron on their way to Glenfinnan, on the west of Loch Eil, where Prince Charlie had that day raised his standard.

Falls on the Spean Roy Bridge

The railway now follows, on the right, the public road that stretches from Fort William to Kingussie, and on the left lies General Wade's military road. Presently Inverlochy Castle, the seat of Lord Abinger, is seen on the right, and at this point a magnificent view is obtained — Loch Linnhe, Loch Eil and the Glenfinnan hills in front and Ben Nevis to the left. Presently the famous Nevis distillery is passed, a building no more picturesque than other distilleries, but which inherits a little romance from the fact that it lies in the shadow of the mighty Ben. It stands on the banks of the Lochy, that river, swelled by the Spean, descending to Loch Linnhe from Loch Lochy. Amongst those who drink that well-known brand of whisky, *Long John,* it is often a source of wonder what the name means, so we give tourists the explanation to carry back to the south. Originally the distillery was a smaller establishment, at Millburn, a few miles off, drawing its water from 1,500 feet up the side of the Ben, and its whisky was named *Dew of Ben Nevis*. Subsequently the present distillery was built (although the old place is still in existence and in full working) drawing its water from Glen Nevis. The distiller was anxious to get a distinctive name for the new whisky, and he hit upon the title *Long John*, as that was the nickname of his grandfather, the original distiller, who was a man six feet four in height.

Just beyond, where the River Lochy pours its waters into Loch Linnhe, stands an old ruin on the bank — the original Inverlochy Castle, a seat of the 'Black Comyns' until they were driven out by Robert the Bruce. According to Mrs MacKellar, "Tradition says that it was built in one night by the Picts, and that their Kings resided there: that King Achaius, who was a contemporary of Charlemagne, signed a treaty there with that monarch, which is still seen among the archives of Paris; and that sixteen gentlemen of the name of Comyn witnessed the treaty". The ruin we now see was certainly not built by the Picts, either in one night or at leisure; we should fix its date in the thirteenth century. Little beyond the four bare walls are now left, with towers at the corners about thirty feet high. The western is known as 'Comyn's Tower', and has walls ten feet thick, while the internal diameter is eight paces, but this tower is larger than the rest. The old keep is picturesquely situated at the water's edge, and must have been a place of great importance in the old days. It was near here that James I of Scotland, in 1429, defeated Alexander, the Lord of the Isles, and Earl of Ross, who had invaded Lochaber with ten thousand men. Two years after, the Islesmen returned under Donald Balloch, again invaded Lochaber, and at Inverlochy utterly defeated the Earls of Mar and Caithness, although numbers were in favour of the Royal leaders.

But the most famous fight at Inverlochy was fought in February, 1645, in the time of the Covenanters, between the Marquis of Montrose — 'the Great Marquis' — on the Royalist side, and the Duke of Argyll for the Covenant. When winter came on, the Duke of Argyll sent his army into winter quarters and retired to his own castle of Inveraray, in fancied security, thinking idly that Montrose could do nothing until spring; but the Marquis, with an army of Highlanders, "wading through drifts of snow, scaling precipices, and traversing the mountain paths, known to none save the solitary shepherd or huntsman", forced an entry into Argyllshire, which he laid waste with fire and

Mallaig junction, start of the stunning Mallaig line.
Below: ready to ride the rail road to the Isles

sword, causing even Argyll himself to flee in a fishing-boat. "Montrose", writes Sir Walter Scott, "continued the work of revenge for nearly a month, and, then concluding he had destroyed the influence which Argyll, by the extent of his power, and the supposed strength of his country, possessed over the minds of the Highlanders, withdrew towards Inverness, with the purpose of organising a general gathering of the clans. But he had scarce made this movement, when he learned that his rival, Argyll, had returned into the Western Highlands with some Lowland forces; that he had called around him his numerous clan, burning to revenge the wrongs which they had sustained, and was lying with a strong force near the old castle of Inverlochy, situated at the western extremity of the chain of lakes, through which the Caledonian Canal is now conducted. The news at once altered Montrose's plans. He returned upon Argyll by a succession of the most difficult mountain passes covered with snow; and the vanguard of the Campbells saw themselves suddenly engaged with that of their implacable enemy. Both parties lay all night on their arms; but, by break of day, Argyll betook himself to his galley, and rowing off shore, remained a spectator of the combat when, by all the rules of duty and gratitude, he ought to have been at the head of his devoted followers. His unfortunate clansmen supported the honour of the name with the greatest courage, and many of the most distinguished fell on the field of battle. Montrose gained a complete victory, which greatly extended his influence over the Highlands, and in proportion diminished that of his discomfited rival."

The hills of Loch Arkaig and of Achnacarry are

seen to the right, the country of the Clan Cameron. By Sir Allan Cameron of Erracht, a cadet of Lochiel, the 79th Cameron Highlanders were raised in the end of the last century. Their achievements have many times been written on the roll of fame, since Byron wrote on Waterloo, "when wild and high the Camerons' gathering rose". The tartan is a beautiful blend of the two clans of the district, Cameron and Macdonald. The Cameron men were once so numerous as to almost justify the strange reply given to a belated but suspected traveller who in a wild night of storm and sleet besought entrance to a solitary house. "Are there no Christians here?" he demanded piteously. "No, no," was the stern answer, "we are all Camerons here."

After passing Inverlochy we enter Fort William — a hundred miles from the start — the railway passing through the old fort, now dismantled, from which the place takes its name. The town is a minute one, with a population of only about 2,000, but it looks quite an imposing city after the wilderness we have come through. The houses struggle along the shore of Loch Linnhe, the wide arm of the sea that stretches up from Mull; but the township is well supplied with hotels; and, as Aunt Gilchrist says in William Black's *In Far Lochaber* — "It's a grand place for being in the middle of things." Now that the West Highland Railway has been constructed, it will be more in the middle of things than ever. The railway, after passing through the fort, runs along an esplanade to the pier, thus making connection with MacBrayne's fine service of steamers, by which the traveller may go south to Oban, and round through the Kyles of Bute to

Craigendoran, whence he started on the West Highland Railway; or will take him north by the beautiful route of the Caledonian Canal to Inverness. For those who come to Fort William by steamer, from either north or south, there is the West Highland to take them east through Lochaber, and south by the route we have traversed, with all its possibilities in the way of diversions to right or left. Apart altogether from its proximity to such notable scenes as Glencoe, Glen Nevis, Glen Finnan, Glen Spean, Glen Roy and Achnacarry, and the fact that it lies at the very base of Ben Nevis, Fort William is certainly "in the middle of things".

The little township has sprung up around the fort, which was originally built by General Monck, in Cromwell's time, as a rude fortification of turf, to act as a base for the troops sent to keep in subjection Evan Dhu of Lochiel, the Chief of the Camerons, who stood out like a Scottish Hereward against the forces of the Commonwealth, long after the other clans had submitted. Many a fierce skirmish between Lochiel and the Sassenach red-coats took place around Fort William and Inverlochy, the Highlanders generally getting the best of it, as is recorded in Scott's *Tales of a Grandfather*. In the time of William the Third the fort was rebuilt in its present form (or rather its late form, for the railway works have cut much of it up) by General Mackay, who was afterwards defeated by Viscount Dundee at Killiecrankie. It was a strong fortification of its kind, with ditch, glacis and ravelin, of which portions may yet be seen, mounting fifteen twelve-pounders and with a regular garrison of about a hundred men: while in times of trouble many more soldiers were thrown into it. Both in the '15 and the '45 it was besieged by the Jacobites, but was never taken. Some interesting particulars of the second siege will be found in Mrs MacKellar's handbook. "There was no village here," says this authority, "previous to the erection of Cromwell's fort. Then some houses began to arise on the face of the hill. Afterwards, when the present fort was built, the people were encouraged to erect houses there, to form a village to be a sutlery to it. They might build where and how they liked, only the houses were to be composed of turf and wattle, so as to be easily set on fire in case of a rising, or of an enemy effecting a lodgment there. This village was demolished, and then the people began to build at the seaside, where the lower streets of the town are now, and the free charters given them accounts for the irregularity of the buildings, which, from the sea, look so disorderly."

Various attempts have been made to re-name the town after it was raised to the dignity of a burgh of barony. First it was called Maryburgh, in honour of William's Consort; but it remained Fort William, in honour of William himself. Later, the Duke of Gordon was made superior of the township, and it was called Gordonsburgh; but it remained Fort William. Afterwards Sir Duncan Cameron became superior, and called it Duncansburgh; but it still remained Fort William. We do not think there is any reason to regret the popular rejection of the three names suggested.

Fort William lies too close to Ben Nevis for a good view of that mountain to be obtained, but the scenery is magnificent without that crowning attraction.

As seen from the Fort William side, Ben Nevis appears a somewhat shapeless mountain, piled shoulder on shoulder, in vast folds of granite into the sky, as if disdaining symmetrical form, and depending on sheer bulk alone to vindicate its grandeur. It is only when it is observed how seldom the summit can be seen free of clouds, that the gigantic height of the Ben is realised (4,406 feet), for it is the highest mountain in the United Kingdom; and it is only when a pedestrian attempts to walk round it, and finds that the base is more than twenty-four miles in circumference, that its colossal bulk is fully grasped. For three-fourths of the ascent the mountain is of red granite, the remaining fourth being of porphyry, "which weathers of a brown colour, but when newly fractured shows bluish and greenish tints, mottled with specks of white felspar."

The ascent may be made either from Fort William or from Banavie, about three miles distant, to which there is a branch line of the West Highland Railway, but the feat should not be attempted without a guide, as the densest of mists descend on the mountain without a minute's warning, and render the position of the mountain climber extremely dangerous. It is proposed to build a railway to the summit, similar to that which ascends the Rigi; but it has not yet got beyond the stage of contemplation.

To reach the summit of Ben Nevis means a climb of five miles up a bridle path, on so steep a gradient that in the distance named there is a rise of over 4,000 feet. This is not a task for a weak-lunged or weak-legged man; but the journey may be partly done on a hill-pony, and at the top there is a small Temperance Hotel, with sleeping accommodation for over a dozen guests, where tea, bed, and breakfast may be obtained for half-a-guinea — a small sum to pay for the proud boast in future years that you have slept on the top of Ben Nevis! The view from the summit is a bewildering one, for the eye looks down on nothing but mountain peaks, except where they are broken by the three great sheets of water — Loch Linnhe, Loch Eil and Loch Lochy, or by the sea itself. To take up again a former simile, it is like standing in the 'ball' of St Paul's, and gazing on the endless miles of the roofs of London, for the hill tops below seem interminable, and might almost be called monotonous in the multitide. On a clear day the eye can trace in the north-east the form of Ben MacDhui, the second mountain in Britain, which rises to a height of 4,296 feet in the Braemar Highlands. To the north the vision ranges as far as Ben Wyvis in Ross-shire. Westward, the Cuillin Hills in Skye may be distinguished, and in particularly favourable weather, some of the heights in the Outer Hebrides, ninety miles away. Southward may be distinguished Ben Cruachan, at the head of Loch Awe, lying almost east of Oban. South-west may be seen the Islands, and even a glimpse of Ireland may be caught. It is a prospect astounding in its wide expanse, and he is lucky who reaches the summit of Ben Nevis on a day when the atmosphere permits of a good view. Frequently the hill-top is shrouded in dense mist, giving on the wall of fog an effect as of the well-known Spectre of the Brocken. On the Ben itself there is a magnificent chasm to be inspected — a perpendicular precipice, ranging from 1,500 to 2,000 feet in depth, which Sir Robert Christison has described as the finest precipice in the world.

On the summit of Ben Nevis is the Observatory, where two meteorologists keep watch on the weather day and night, summer and winter, watch and watch about, so that hourly readings of the instruments may be taken, and telegraphed to the low-level Observatory at the base of the hill in Fort William.

The Observatory was opened in 1883, but has been considerably enlarged since, and now presents the appearance of a primitive fort, surmounted at one end by a watch tower thirty feet high. It is provisioned for nine months, as it is frequently cut off for many weeks at a time from all communication with the world below, while even in the middle of summer the transport of stores is no easy task. As an indication of what the life is of the two lonely observers, we quote a passage from a pamphlet on the subject — "The most unpleasant weather is when it rains while the temperature is still below freezing. The rain then freezes as it falls, and everything gets covered with hard ice, which may increase in thickness indefinitely, the only limit being the time that these conditions continue. On one occasion it lasted for two days, and the ice was more than a foot thick, both on the ground and on the windward side of all projections . . . During the months of February and March it is not uncommon to have south-easterly gales blowing for three or four days continuously, at the rate of eighty to a hundred miles an hour; but under these circumstances the hill-top is usually swept at once clear of all loose snow, and a hard surface of rough ice left, on which good footing may be got. At first, when the surface was icy, and the wind very strong, the observers used to go out roped together, but experience has shown that even in the most violent gusts, safety may be got by lying down. . . . On the night of the 21st of February, 1885, a terrific southerly gale blew with hurricane force, and stopped all outside observation for fifteen hours. It was impossible to stand or even to crawl to windward, while the most carefully shielded lantern was blown out at once. During the height of the gale the air was full of snowdrift, intermixed with which were great lumps of hardened snow that had been torn from the ground by the violence of the wind. One of these flying pieces broke the only window that was above the snow." *

It is from Banavie (pronounced with the accent on the first syllable), about three miles north-east of Fort William, lying on the Caledonian Canal, that the best view of Ben Nevis may be obtained, and to Banavie there is, as we have said, a short branch line of the West Highland Railway. The position of Banavie at the junction of Loch Eil and Loch Linnhe — giving magnificent views each way — and its uniformly bright aspect, forces the impression that among the earliest developments which the railway communication will ensure, will be the growing importance of this favourably placed village as a tourist centre for the Mid-Western Highlands.

Leaving Fort William, the line crosses the Lochy at Old Inverlochy Castle, and traverses the bare Corpach Moss, to the side of the Canal, where the famous 'Neptune's Staircase' is to be seen, the

* For a full account of life on the Ben, see Ben Nevis and its Observatory, *also from Northern Books.*

grand finale of the artificial water-way. It consists of eight locks, end to end, each with a drop of eight feet of water, so that a vessel entering the chain changes its level sixty-four feet before it resumes sailing in the open. The delay is, of course, considerable: but the tourist has no reason to grumble, for he finds close by 'Neptune's Staircase' an exceedingly comfortable hotel — the 'Lochiel Arms', which has bedroom accommodation for over a hundred guests. From the windows he has the fine view of Ben Nevis, of which we have spoken. From this point of view the form of the mountain is majestic in the extreme, and its contour may be traced from the radiant heather-clad base to the snow-capped summit lost in the clouds. An amusing anecdote is told by Mrs MacKellar, who writes, "It is said that the ancient charter, by which the proprietor of the mountain held his land, gave him it as long as there was snow on Ben Nevis, and that one year so little snow had fallen in winter, and the summer was so hot, that he had to put a tent over a snow-wreath to keep it from melting, lest his tenure of the land would be gone." It is seldom such a precaution is necessary!

As a souvenir of Banavie, we may give the tourist the explanation of why a lobster is known in the West Highlands as a 'Banavie Flea'. A good many years ago an American was stopping in the Banavie hotel, and he made himself very obnoxious by his contemptuous remarks on Scottish scenery. "Ben Nevis?" he said; "do you call that a mountain? You should see our mighty Rockies! Loch Linnhe? Do you call that a lake? You should see our Lake Superior! Rannoch Moor? Do you call that a plain?

BEWARE
OF
TRAINS

you should see our western prairies!" and so he went on, to the intense exasperation of the Highland waiter, who went and procured a live lobster (for they are caught occasionally in the Loch) which he secreted, in requital of the insults, in the American's bed. Hardly had the American gone to sleep when the lobster caught him by the toe with a grasp like a vice. He jumped out of bed with a yell and rang for the boots. "Boots," he said solemnly, rubbing his toe as he spoke, "you may not have such big mountains and big lakes and big plains here as we have in the States, but you have the most tarnation big fleas I ever experienced."

A Banavie Flea

From Fort William there are various attractive day trips, one of the most notable being up Glen Nevis, along which a coach runs for about six miles. The Glen is a very wild and picturesque one, threaded by the crystal waters of the River Nevis, and used to be a favourite pasture for goats, which found in the precipices a congenial home. At Achariach, about six miles up, beyond the Druidical 'rocking-stone' and the ancient vitrified fort are the Lower Falls of Nevis, a beautiful cascade, and a mile further on is one of the most striking waterfalls in the Kingdom, a stream foaming down the side of

Ben Nevis at an angle of about sixty degrees, for a distance of about 1,000 feet. After passing a cave, about which there is some very curious folklore, a rough walk of about two miles brings the traveller to the Upper Falls of Nevis, which have a stupendous drop of about 500 feet, not unlike that of the Falls of Foyers.

Another enjoyable trip is up Glenfinnan, seventeen miles, to the spot where Prince Charlie raised his standard in the '45; going along Loch Eil to Glenfinnan, passing by the old house — Fassifern — long the residence of Sir Ewan Cameron, the gallant soldier who was killed while commanding his regiment at Quatre Bras. A monument now marks the spot — "more like an old lighthouse than anything else," as the writer of Baddeley's Guide aptly says, crowned by a figure of the Prince himself, looking up the Glen for the Camerons, who had been delayed by the skirmish at Highbridge we mentioned before. At Fassifern Prince Charlie spent a night of his weary wanderings on his way to the safe shelter on Ben Alder. From the ramparts too, we can see across the Loch near Banavie, a spot which preserves the memory of Shakespeares's murdered Banquo, Thane of Lochaber. It is called 'Banquo's walk'. His son Fleance fled to Brittany, whence his descendants returned in the train of William the Conqueror, and later to their native land as the Stuart Kings of Scotland. Lochaber is thus the cradle of our Royal race. Yet another tempting drive is, twelve and a half miles to the 'Dark Mile of Achnacary', a magnificent avenue of trees, like a cathedral aisle, the branches joining and forming an umbrageous roof.

But to sketch the attractions that lie around Fort William would be an endless task. In whatever direction the traveller sets out he will be thoroughly satisfied with the day's experience when he returns to his hotel at night.

Mairi Hedderwick's

Views of Scotland

A classic collection of enchanting scenes from one of the country's most talented illustrators

Northern Books
from Famedram

Ben Nevis and its Observatory

A guide to the Ben and to the Observatory built on the summit in 1883

Northern Books
from Famedram